BLOOD MUSIC

Frank Reardon

Punk ♪ Hostage ♪ Press

Blood Music
Frank Reardon

ISBN-13: 978-1940213903
ISBN-10: 1940213908

Punk Hostage Press
P.O. Box 1869
Hollywood CA 90078

www.punkhostagepress.com

Introduction by John Dorsey

Cover Design by SB Stokes

Edited by A. Razor

Some of These Poems Appear In

GREEN PANDA PRESS
BLUE HOUR MAGAZINE
THE IDIOM
EPIC RITES PRESS
MY FAVORITE BULLET
UNSHOD QUILLS
LUMMOX PRESS
BOLD MONKEY
NEW MEXICO REVIEW

Editor's Acknowledgments

On an evening of Santa Ana winds blowing through Echo Park I received a call from S.A. Griffin about going to see a poet who was visiting Los Angeles a few years back. The poet was Frank Reardon, whose latest book you are now about to read, and he was holed up temporarily in a North Hollywood apartment where he was staying with Jason Neese and his fiancé (now wife) Amelie Florence, during a trip through area. I had read Frank's work on the internet and in a book he had recently put out of his work which S.A. had let me borrow to read.

S.A. did these things all the time, being an ambassador and host of the L.A. literary scene that Iris and I had been raised up in as well. The opportunity to sit and talk with writers who I had an admiration for was something I was hungry to do at the time. I had spent about 15 years fairly isolated from any literary interaction and was just starting to connect with people again and discover more about the literary network that had developed along with the internet during my absence.

Frank Reardon sat across from me at a kitchen table and we all spoke of many things that all involved the creative process and the awkward feelings that we both shared about the process of sharing the work with others, being a part of a greater community and such. After that night I followed Frank's work more closely than I had before. Communicating about the connectivity between writing and life with Frank over the last few years has been inspiring, to say the least. It is easy to see why I was excited when Frank agreed to work on a book with Iris and myself.

Punk Hostage Press has grown since its inception on January 13, 2012 to encompass a wide variety of literary approaches that have one common ground that is shared among them. They are all books that Iris and I have loved as much as the authors of the books have loved them. This shared emotional draw to the work at hand has made it possible for us to see the things in the work that the writer sees through their eyes and share the vision for the book all the way through the process. Without really ever being cognizant of it, I had been preparing for this work my whole life and it is only since we first made this commitment to publishing that I began to see the real fruits of all those years spent reading and writing and breaking it all down. Hopefully my efforts have served Frank Reardon's *Blood Music* well enough for this relationship to be felt by the reader as well.

Blood Music by Frank Reardon is very poignant slice of this writer's life blood made into works that can be shared with his readership in a way that we feel has the integrity that this work deserves. Punk Hostage Press is proud to be a part of the presentation of his work and we have to acknowledge all the work that went into this collection to make the final outcome possible.

First, we would want to extend our grateful thanks to April Michelle Bratten for her editing and proofing of the first manuscript as well as the support she has been giving to Punk Hostage Press since we released our first book in 2012.

Next, to the esteemed peers who gave the quotable feedback for this book, Dan Fante, Moriah LaChapell Shalock, Lawrence Gladview and James H. Duncan, we are forever indebted to your supportive words.

Also, there is the relevant and touching Introduction by our friend John Dorsey, who has created a portal to this book that is nothing short of perfect.

The cover art is from the efforts of my colorful dream states to be deciphered, understood and rendered into a beautiful clarity by SB Stokes in order for him to create an impressive finish to this book.

I humbly hope that this book is the vehicle of a great voyage into the contemporary poetics of a world that demands a certain amount of sacrifice for the only reward we have come to understand as meaningful: a real purpose for art as love as blood as demonstrated in this process that is relative to living and surviving in order to dance once more to this sacred music that has been created among us.

- A. Razor 2013

Introduction

The first time I met Frank Reardon I wasn't sure I liked him, but I was fairly certain that the poetry reading we were at wasn't worth either of our time. That was 2008 on a little roller coaster ride known as the Connecticut Beat Poetry—my head is still spinning from all the tough guy bullshit and the Beards mumbo jumbo. The one good thing that came out of that whole period was the friendships that were made that week.

At first glance I thought Frank was just another tough kid from Boston who worshipped at the altar of Charles Bukowski and Jack Kerouac and maybe he was. Over the years though, I've seen Frank grow as both an artist and a human being and as a friend. If you've followed Frank's work since the beginning, I think that evolution has been clearly spelled out in verse.

All of this leads me to his latest collection, "Blood Music." I'll just say it, I liked these poems. They feel like a Dylan melody. Even the title seems to be one of reflection, one of quiet devotion to the craft and beauty of just being alive and looking toward the future. It's clear to me that Frank is simply more comfortable in his own skin.

Some of the best moments in this book are the briefest, seen in poems like "For Bill Gainer" and "Badlands Death Haiku." This book is all about those tiny moments of revelation and the decisions we make both good and bad and just owning up to our place in the world.

Others talk of poetry, love, and family, such as Frank's touching poem for his daughter "Ship in the Bottle." I'll admit that this poem nearly made me tear up, as I know a bit about Frank's family history, but I think that anyone would be touched by the honesty here.

Lastly, I think this book is about nature, human and otherwise. It's about the author's surroundings--including his heart. Yes, that's there too, on full view for everyone to see.

All of this is my longwinded way of saying that maybe I had Frank all wrong from the very beginning. There is no posing here, only a confident stillness that comes with age. Frank no longer has to compete with the dead or this week's literary internet sensation, only himself, and as he runs toward the sun, I hope to be there to hand him a beer and just maybe Brian Hardie will be there to hand us both some Burger King. And I only wish I had a reply to Frank's letter to me, but I'm not that deep, and besides, I hope we have a while before we both have to figure it all out.

So if you think you know Frank Reardon, well, I'm just asking you to not judge a book by its cover, unless of course, you happen to be holding a copy of "Blood Music." Then by all means, dance yourself silly under the stars.

-John Dorsey, Author of *Tombstone Factory,*
Epic Rites Press, 2013.

This book is dedicated to Lillian Grace Reardon.

Contents

"Suddenly I realize
That if I stepped out of my body I would break
Into blossom. "
— James Wright.

Heavy in the Dirt

as the hiking boots
finally learn
to bend
more
than the spine
of a book,
I too
will not
look into the eyes
of man
until the
 ego goes
blind.

Sometimes it Gets So Bad That Our Failures Are All We've Got Left to Celebrate

We arrived in Pittsburgh
at 2 a.m.
It was always
2 a.m. in Pittsburgh.

The bus driver
told us
that we could smoke
inside of the cage,

& like the cow
before
the sledgehammer,
we slowly filed
inside
& lit our cigarettes
in unison.

We stood in different
sections
of the cage,
said nothing
to one another,
with our head-clouds
of smoke
& glowing cherries.

I thought
about what day
or time I would arrive
in Huntsville.

I thought about

my ex-wife
& how she couldn't
care less that I lived
on buses,

how she gladly
counted out
the last money
I had sent her
the week before,

how she laughed
out loud
because I lived off
of Slim Jims
& how everything
I owned
was inside
of one suitcase,

how she mocked me
to her friends
& the universe
because I was off
in the world
writing poetry,
trying to find
a voice,
& how I was going
to be a huge
failure.

Then an old woman,
who smelled
like a bag of shit
left on a porch

for 4 days,
asked me for
a cigarette.

I gave her one
& she continued
to stand
next to me
for what seemed
like an eternity.

The smell got so bad
that I began
to celebrate it.

When the bus driver
finally called out
for us to return
to the bus in 5 minutes,
I lit another one.

I gave the shit
stinking lady
another one too.

I leaned
into her smell,
as if half of me
was inside of another
dimension,
& lit the cigarette
for her.

She thanked
me with a nod,
& while we watched

all the people
 inside the cage
stomp out their cigarettes
with a nervous frenzy
& rush for the bus
so they would
not be left behind,
the smelly old lady
looked up
into the Pittsburgh
sky, blew out
a huge cloud
of smoke & said:

"Thank god
we still
have the stars."

Monotony

as the rabbit stares at me
with her deep black
eyeballs,

as the man upstairs
screams
at his 5 year old boy
for spilling his juice,

as a teacher teaches
another bored student
the importance
& impact of Shakespeare,

as the young girl
across the street
changes
in front of her window,

as the gods parade down the
street, waving
their flags
& shooting their guns,

as a monk eats
one grain
of rice,

as the trashcan
overflows
outside my
window,

one piece of the puzzle

waits,
one piece
with many different
colors & shapes,

 & out of all
of the pieces
you've had the patience
to fit
into place,

you still wait,
rubbing together
the final sides, hoping,
that this time
you'll
get it right.

At Vesuvio's

if there was ever
a moment,
ever a time,
when we began cutting
away at the barbwire
surrounding
the heart,
 it was after
we ordered
our first drink.
 it was after
we learned to speak
from the shady
side of our ribs.

Butte

from up high on the butte
i can see all
4 of them,

the little boy,
the egotistical writer,
the priest,
the drunk.

they're crying & wondering
if i'll ever come back down,

but the more i sweat,
breathe,
& fasten my pack,

the more their tears
turn into rage.

we won't follow you, they yell,
while throwing rocks
of old memories at me.

you'll come back,
you always do!
you'll never be able
to do it on your own!

they start to offer me
all the things
that had once kept me
from moving.

accepting nothing

but everything,
i look out into the world
from atop the butte,

miles upon miles
of horizon,
the world meeting me
from all 4 directions,

taking the first step.

It Has Been a Year or Two

it has been a year
or two now
of weekly walks
through the park
to get to my
shrink's office

where I no longer
take it upon myself
to drink for all
the different
voices & personas
that have been
jamming up
my head

all those many
years
completely unaware
& drunk 7 days
a week

finally whittled down
to one voice
one human
one pair
of hiking boots

& with each step
that I continue
to take

I can finally taste
the flowers

in the wind

I can finally bring
together silence's
two giant iron hands

wrap them
around my head
& juice out
every last voice
with my tears.

A Letter to John Dorsey

John,

I didn't know that the streets climbed up into the sky.
If that's a given, I must insist on tucking my knees in
on the way up.
& when it's your turn, I know that you'll snap your fingers
with a rhythmic beat,
just like the doo-wop boys did during their West Side Story
knife fight, but do we take poems with us?
Not the every-day-zen ones, but the ones that Ruggles shouted
at the lifeguard, or the ones that Hardung whispered to the ants
on his private hill in Kansas City?

I figure, John, that astral projections are useless & inadequate,
especially when it's reality that becomes the one to undress us.
& I don't expect for us to hear the foot kicking against the inside
of the trunk, but we were built to be heroes, & I'm not talking
about Steve McQueen, or the Argonauts,
but the kind of heroes that love women like thermonuclear war,
the kind of heroes that stick roses between the teeth of death.

& all of this chatter about the 'Old Midnight Angel' from Lowell
& the angry postman from Los Angeles is growing stagnant.
It's not that they're any less than miracles, but they no longer
create new ones, not to mention, I expect that most symbols
grow tired of themselves, at least when the screaming mob sticks
a finger inside of its pocket & pretends that it carries a big gun.

I remember how we shouldered looks from rare girls
with the laughter of a Berryman suicide all the way down
to the ground & out of nowhere, looking like a couple of
overdrawn one-liners, but those ice cold beers down
on the corner of Prospero's were magnificent,

our faces like children pawing at ice cream,
while those girls spoke tight denim languages with hair
of sexual freedom,
& I saw how you watched their asses pull the string.
How alert the world had become back then,
how that flick of the tongue against the front tooth created
a spark,
how one word of need behaved like a firecracker.

Consider this for a moment, John.
Human blood is not pale. It's bright, bright on the inside,
bright when it falls out of us, bright when lightning hits it,
& as bright as Wannberg's cherub laughter.

We learned this in a Hartford biker bar
with old wooden tables that had trouble holding
up our words,
with its bartender of monk-like-joy,
with its pool table where Lester Allen dropped Vicodin
down his throat.

I was bashful back then, hiding my baby face in the rings
 of a pint,
spitting breakfast words to a dinner crowd, but you were
there, sitting back in your full beard of massive sorrow,
waiting for the birds to break the back
of an everyday feeling.

This is not to say that California will not ever fall off
the map due to an earthquake, & this is not to say that
floating in orbit creates a scandal, it's just to say that
 'being' is what it is,
& anything else feels like a lie.

We've become a world of sages without followers,
we've become hearts without minds,

& we've become skeletons without tendons, but you
always knew
that it takes a huge amount of sweat, elbow grease,
& agony to get there.

Besides, John, how good would greatness feel
without failure first?

& how could we even know what failure felt like
if we didn't get up & try living in the first place?

Unmovable Fragrance

Troubled by wine,
       unaware of the darkening skies
that poured down from the highway of nightmare lands,
       with consciousness   fermenting
in traces of moonlight's footsteps,
      you would bark
        as a mad dog,
      looking for the simple & the blessed
that lived as fragrance floating within strange truths,
     that dressed in the temples of empty skies.
      You would banish these immortal gods,
stripping them down
      to the plain lotus,
       sucking them up into the unmovable *void*
chanting with the words
         of twinkling stars,
     exploding viciously into the unseen ending,
     locating the core of silence
and then, with a river of wind,
          Laughter.

The Poet & His Ponytail

He liked to stand up at readings,
wave his arms around, & golf clap
to get people's attention.

"This next piece is from my Pulitzer
nominated collection of
poetry titled, *Simple Beach Winds
Blowing Across My Balls.*"

When the poem ended,
the entire crowd
(with their index fingers & thumbs
holding up their heads)
breathed a collective sigh
that blew gently across
the poetic atmosphere.

"This next poem is from my
Pushcart nominated book
titled, *Kittens Churning Butter
in the Stables of Lost Love.*"

Before he started to read,
he threw his ponytail
over his denim shirt,
sipped from his wine spritzer,
& looked directly into
the eyes of the crowd.

Wives fell in love,
husbands cried with envy,
tons of cameras flashed,
children waited for autographs,
old women unbuttoned the

tops of their blouses,
old men thought
of themselves
wearing suede boots.

"This next poem is from
my Best of the Net
nominated book titled,
It's Simply Sunday Morning
Coffee in the Time of Chaucer."

& just before he finished the poem,
he let out a huge scream,
pounded on his chest,
& exclaimed "I am the Poet!
I am the one they call the 3rd dawn!"

Champagne tops popped off,
someone screamed *Bravo*!
women fainted,
a dog humped the leg of a chair,
death got on the phone & said,
"Did you hear that?...I quit!"

Then, there was me,
& hopefully you too,
forever working
& waiting on the words
to find us first.

Soon Enough

arranged in the dark,
naked,
& without purpose,

her hands,
like broken pieces of porcelain,
study, count,
& caress
the lines
of my aging
face

just as the prisoner
would do
with the lines
in his
cinder block wall.

it was only
a matter of time
until
it all added
up.

For **Bill Gainer**

On midnight twinkle
of Christmas tree
light,
I found him
hanging there,
the world glowing haiku

Competing With the Dead

I skinned
my boxing gloves
& buried the punches deep
into the soil

no funeral,
no weeping,
or goodbyes

there were just two
bare naked
hands

that quickly
stitched together
a new pair
of hiking boots
made from
the leftover skins

& much like
the eyelets
of the gloves

the laces
of the boots
were drawn up
so tight

that the dead
never had
a chance
 to breathe.

Badlands Death Haiku

trapped finch whistles
in the ceiling of the barn,
you think it's easy?

It Will Come Out of Nowhere Like a Gunshot

turning the bends
of the trail,

walking the ups
& downs,

the bees in front of me
are just bees,

the hanging limbs
of the trees
are touching
nothing,

the sweat on my
neck is only
sweat,

the flowers
are red, yellow
& purple,

they stand only
because of their roots
& the act of soil,

the wild turkey
runs away
from me, because
it's a turkey,

the duck slaps
his feathers

against the emptiness
of the water,

& when the trail
turns into the park
with its screaming children,
& disheveled
looking parents,
my shoulders grow tight,
my head becomes dizzy,

I keep walking
through everything
but nothing,

reminding myself
of a line
from the 'Diamond Sutra':

Even the words
'total Enlightenment'
are merely words,

feet move on,
the trail is still
only a trail,
& the thoughts in my mind
are just thoughts,
not unlike
the scattering of birds
after a gunshot.

Elephant

there was a time
when the poems
meant nothing,
said nothing.

bizarre word pairings
for no reason
other than putting
them together.

some people proclaimed:
"genius,"
or "brilliant,"
so, i kept writing them.

i kept letting the cheers
fill my head.
i kept drinking gallons
of liquor & spewing the silly words.

then, one day,
i woke up with a hangover
that would have killed
an elephant.

my head pounded,
my body shook
like a box of nails.

it was so bad
that even my ego
had abandoned me.

it was just me, alone

with the sickness,
& there was no moment
that defined change.

there was no sun shining
through the window
that made me decide
to move on.

there was no choir of birds
on the telephone wire
that called for my death.

there was no punch to the jaw
from a bar fight
after a night of whiskey
& whores.

it was just me,
it was just as it was,

just the self,
coming out of a long coma,
having to relearn
to pound the keyboard,
having to relearn
the truth that was hiding
inside the brain.

it was simple, really,
like looking at a mountain,
like calling your child
on the phone,
like playing a favorite record.

now, the "genius"

& "brilliant" labels
have vanished.

the struggle
to constantly put out material
that was full of lies
is all but gone.

they call me dull now,
just another old man
without guts
walking nature trails,
& sitting on benches.

just another traitor
who gave up on being a "poet."

Ship in the Bottle

there were too many mistakes
& too many lawyers.
i did not want you to see me
as the tear inside that old bottle,
trying so hard to rebuild the old ship,
trying so hard to be your father.

The Bell

All it took
to put me on the couch
for an entire year
was someone saying,
"50 on pump 5."

I felt my hands
go numb,
I went dizzy,
& the fear took
me over.

I left my cash register,
walked out the door,
& got in my car,
leaving a line
of customers inside.

My mind became its own mind
as I drove past the children
playing outside,
the blooms falling
from the trees,
the sun shining
on bikini girls
lounging in their
front yard.

I got to my house,
went inside,
sat on the couch,
& said nothing
to anyone,
letting the first tears

of my adult life
roll from my eyes.

Nothing dramatic
happened.
There was no hold up
in the store,
no gang land slayings,
or people getting
arrested.

There was no high stakes
poker game,
no mafia hits,
no outlaws riding
off into the sunset.

Losing one's mind
happens
during the turning
of a radio station,
or after putting on underwear
& noticing that they're on
backwards.

It happens
while petting your rabbit
& your voice
turns into a child's voice.
It goes when you look
into the mirror
& see the black bags
under your eyes.

It happens
as you look out

into the store
& see the line
of people holding
their sodas
& gas money.

It happens
after you punch
in the numbers
to your register,
its loud bell
signaling to you
that a drawer
is about to fly open.

5 ft 1 & Shitting Railroad Tracks

At 5 ft 1 you drank more than anyone I had ever seen.
You'd turn the bottle of Heaven Hill
upside down & take massive gulps
until it was gone. I would stay in the corner,
scribbling secret notes & playing music.

You liked it when I wrote.
You never wanted to hear any of the poems,
but my madness coming out on paper
in between sips of beer,
somehow calmed you down.

That was before you put my face into the dashboard
in the head-on collision on Slaughter Rd.,
before your weekly religious conversions,
before the mind games & jealous trickery.

Those days, in the trailer,
we only had two nickels to rub together for bread.
I had to walk 3 miles to work
because we drank the gas money,
& you slept until 4 p.m. with a hangover
as I wrote in the other room
with black coffee & my own hangover,
two metal pans slapping against my head.

Those were the days of passion
& reality. Those were the times
when I could count on something happening,
anything to keep the fires burning.

When I think of all that madness
that I endured

while trying to find my voice,
while working at the Coke plant,
while dealing with all your rabbit punches,
I am reminded of how thick
my skin was, how much I was made of iron.

Nowadays,
it's shrinks,
walks in the park,
& observing the birds.
Yes, these things are necessary now,
but my confidence was unbreakable
back then, unshakable.

You used to tell me that
I owned any room that I stood in,
that my head was always high,
& even if a man knocked me down
he still lost the fight.

I pissed nails & shit railroad tracks
you'd say,
& I often felt that way,
even after your religious conversion,
even after the divorce.

I felt that way when I lived on Greyhound buses,
inside the dark bars of Kansas City,
Decatur county, & West Warwick,
when I was camping in abandon houses,
& seedy hotels with loose women
who claimed to like what I wrote,
but never understood a line of it.

It only made me stronger
when you'd get so drunk & punch me,

& with each black eye,
with each cut, or bloody nose,
I'd believe in the world even more.

It made me realize that all the writing
was the right thing to do,
as you dressed the wounds
that you inflicted on my face.

I saw it all before me, there for the taking,
when you put a cold beer
on my eye
& slowly blew your liquor breath
onto the scabs that had
already formed,
but this was all before you found some god
while picking up
beer bottles from under the bed.

At first I thought it was a sick joke
until you tried to force me into joining,
until I came home from work
& noticed that all my books were in the trash,
until you began to punch me
for all the wrong reasons,
like not mowing the grass,
& drinking on Sunday.

The magic ended when I crossed
the t's on the divorce papers.
All those hard nights
& beer soaked days were down the toilet,
all that class & reality you once had,
gone within seconds,
like a side of beef tossed to the dogs.

With that Jesus shirt you wore,
you told me that I was shit,
& for a few years I was.
You told me that I was doomed to fail,
that I'd be nothing,
& for a few years I was,
but it all began to make sense
during those hateful nights,
with all those women with vaginal warts
inside the vacant hotels of my heart.

Now there are books,
5 sold, 10, 25, 100...
Now there are readings,
radio shows,
& delusional nights by the machine.

Sometimes I think about you
when I write,
how at 5 ft 1
with your bottle in hand,
you gave me your special gift,

& I still have it,
& I'll use it when no one is looking,
because an isolated rage
that powerful,
& a fire that burns that wild,
& roams that out of control,
should never be in the hands of a novice.

The Saint Card on My Nightstand

at 8 years old
i'd have these terrible
nightmares
of being buried alive i
nside of coffins.

i'd claw & bang
at the lid
trying to find
my way out,
but as always
it was useless,

until, one night,
i awoke crying
in my bed.

my grandmother
ran in
& asked
"what is wrong?"

"i don't wanna die,"
i told her.

reaching into her
nightgown pocket,
she pulled out
a Padre Pio card
& placed it on my
night stand.

"this will protect you
whenever you're scared,"

she said.
"just read the prayer
out loud on the back
of the card."

every night after that
i slept next to the mad
white bearded saint
who gazed at me
from my night stand,

his head surrounded
by a blazing yellow sun,

his hands wrapped
in bandages
from the wounds
of the stigmata.

on the back of the card
it mentioned
that his wounds
smelled of roses,

& they'd bleed
right through
the bandages
each time he received
the Eucharist.

i had always felt a strange
but strong connection
with old Pio's picture
when i was a child,

& all these years later

i still carry the same picture
of him
 in my wallet,

& at night
after the writing
is finished
& the pages
are stained,

i take him out
of my wallet
when no one is looking
& whisper to him,

"i'm still bleeding through
these bandages too, Pio,
but the smell
of all these roses
finally filling up my room
has made it worthwhile."

Looking Out the Window

it is snowing in Minot, North Dakota,
& I can hear the trains down
at the bottom of the hill
with their wheels that grind cold steel,
with whistles that blow nonchalantly,
signaling to passengers to climb aboard
for Fargo, Minneapolis, & Chicago

& inside my mind she's older now,
hair longer, heart bigger;
she's curious about grasshoppers
& angry that the candy is all gone,
she likes to trace her hand onto paper
so she can laugh at the crooked outlines
of her fingertips

a man had warned me about this once;
how too much thinking at the windowsill
will drive one into fits of hysteria, but
i have always been fond of the unknown,
fond of being the only living witness
to the deep & impressionable lines
of a breathy hand print
pressed against
a winter window.

The Crash

the dark afternoon sky,

lonely liquor bottles
giving color
to the bar,

men trying
to forget
their angry wives,

it's all
the same;

the ashtrays
of the world
full of butts,

the barking dogs
inside the head
of a hangover,

the pain
of black coffee
in the stomach,

the shrink
saying
the same goddamned
thing over
& over,

the bashful flowers
hiding

inside the heart,

love lining
the thickness
of the skull,

the starving footprints
in the snow
left by the wild cats
at the backdoor,

it's all
the same;

the black rings
of creeping death
inside the bathtub,

never ending
piles
of dishes
blowing OCD
kisses,

a symphony of pills
to cure
the silence,

no cards or letters
in the mailbox,
just bills
without the money,

too many poems, too much prose,
pounding the keys,
trying to find

a voice
of running water
to calm the flames,

no cause,
no reason,

too many broken spines
& pages piled up
around the house;
the greatest trick
ever known,

wondering if a fresh coat
of paint
will fix the yellow
stained walls,

children praying
that their parents
are who they say
they are,

guilt by the crack
of the whip
& relief by the kick
of the boot,

short steps
into the bathroom
where it looks
the same
as the parlor
& kitchen,

long hallways

without paintings
at the end,

long roads
without nirvana;

if i ever tried to sleep
it off,
i would sleep
for eternity.

Poolside

there was a time,
most recently,
when i feared death;

i'd check my calves hourly
for blood clots,
using a tape measure
to make sure
that they were both
the same size.

i'd look to see if my finger nails
were blue.
i'd check my pulse
& blood pressure
every hour
for a possible heart attack.

if dizziness occurred
with ringing in the ears
combined with a headache,
i was convinced
that it was a brain aneurysm.

but what made death laugh
the most,
what made him realize
he had me right where
he wanted me,

was the time i was down
on my knees
in front of the toilet.

that's what it had come to,
all those years
of pain & madness,
had me hysterically
gripping
my very own shit
as i looked for signs of blood,

blood that was never there.

& it was not the shrinks
of the world,
or the multi-colored pills
that pulled me up
from my knees,
nor was it some 'god,'
or mantra,

it was the snow falling
on the pines,

the rabbit that bounced
around the living room,

the book that i was writing,
the music that i listened to.

it was the tea i made
on the hot stove,

it was the small hikes
that i took in the woods,

it was the tears of self-realization
that washed away

the shit stains
from my hands.

now,
death has taken a small vacation,
& even though he'll always be present,
for the time being
he's wearing Bermuda shorts
& sitting poolside
with an umbrella drink.

everything else?
boundless,
enduring,
& deathless,

nothing more than a series of stories
that can do no more
than strike a little bit
of fear
into the hearts
of our children,

it's all i ever asked for.

U.S. Route 72 Memphis to Huntsville

like the sawdust Beale St.
tequila rooms

& like the slide guitar
skirts
hiking up around
the thighs
of the universe

the high speeds
of a 3 a.m.
Mississippi moon
is a giant peach

waiting for me
to reach out
& put my heart

on repeat

Opening the Veins of Youth

the old poet sat
drinking coffee,
staring out
the window,
& opening his veins
like he'd always
done before

the young poet came in
& sat next
to him
& said
"I don't need to
read any
of those
dead guys.
I'm alive,
that's
all that matters!"

the old poet
said nothing,
his once
young & vibrant
blue eyes
now wrinkled
& wise,
as he continued to
watch the birds
dance around
the branches
& the squirrels
dig in the ground,

for no reason
other than
it's just
what he did

"did you not
hear me?"
the young poet
asked.
"I don't need
to read
the stuff
you told me
to read.
I don't need
any of it.
I just need
to know
that I am
alive!
besides,
I have
a new chapbook
out now
& the girls
love it.
I'm rubbing
up against
fame now,
so who needs
any of those
guys?
they don't
know the streets,
or how 'I'
feel inside."

the old poet
continued
to look out
the window
while he rubbed
the pain out
of his arthritic
fingers.
then with
a large sigh
through
his nose,
he got up,
walked
to his toolbox,
& placed
the razor
he normally
used to open
up his veins,
& put it
back inside,
closed it
tight, &
locked it up.

"did you hear
me?"
the young poet
asked, again.
"I am on
the cusp
of fame with
my new
chapbook!"

still saying
nothing,
the old poet
opened his
window
& climbed out.
the singing
birds
were all
that he could
handle.
it's all he ever
wanted
to handle.

The King of Decatur City

The judge entered the room.
He looked like a weasel of a man,
and I imagined that he had just finished
humping his court reporter in his chambers,
her skirt pulled up over her head
as he fucked her with his black robe still on,
his pressed pants down and around his ankles.
He probably even blew his load in front of
the smiling face of George Bush hanging
on the wall.

One by one, he read out our names,
McGuire,
Soto,
Jenkins...

and each one, in short-shackled steps
walked up to his bench.
A discussion would ensue for a few minutes
as the crowd looked on with anger.

Muldoon!? he shouted.

In 2004 you had a fine for $150,
now its $375. How do you plea?

Guilty, I said.

When can you pay? he asked,
as he looked over my arrest sheet
and tapped his pen, waiting to
write something down.

In about three weeks, when I am working.

Alright then, three weeks. If you don't pay
and I see you back here,
it will be 10 days in Huntsville.

He called out another name, and I was shuffled out
and put in line with the others.

We short-stepped back into the van,
and as we headed back to Decatur
for our release,
the guards played music
and smoked cigarettes.

There was much joy in the van
as we all talked.
Someone mentioned his girlfriend,
another talked about Christmas,
and another guy said he was going to Memphis
for work. It was the best
20 minute car ride of my life,
and I didn't want to lose the feeling.

After our release, Soto handed out cigarettes,
and we stood on the corner
in our street clothes and smoked them.
It was 7 men enjoying a simple victory together.
The battle was over.
We could now go home, victorious.

I held my head high like a great champion
as I walked those first few miles.
I even skipped a few times.
This was it, I thought,

the feeling of winning,
the feeling of never going back,
the feeling of a proud man.

I grew more and more tired
while I walked over a bridge, but
the Tennessee river was beautiful that day.
It had a light fog over the water
that was pinkish from the sun,
and when I kicked some pebbles
so I could watch the fish jump,
a little old lady pulled over.

You need a ride? she asked.

Knowing I had ten miles left to go,
I got in.

I did not say much, but
I listened to her stories
about her son,
and how she was so proud of him
for building a ramp
so the handicapped could go to church
and sing.

I felt like singing too.

She dropped me off at the Madison line
where there was a Waffle House.
Instead of calling a friend so I could have
a bed for the night,
I went inside.

I ordered the biggest hot coffee
and the largest stack of pancakes that I could.

I made no noise and said nothing
to anyone
as I ate the meal of a king.

When I was finished,
I leaned back,
unbuttoned my pants,
and lit a cigarette.

As I smoked, I thought
about happy Soto
and the old lady.

I noticed that there was some
hot syrup left on my chin, but
I let it stay where it was
as a reminder,

at least until I left.

An Alabama Divorce

After she had left you,
after she had taken everything,
after the blood in the veins
turned to ice,
& the wind in the lungs
turned to steel,
there is nothing left.

Nothing left
but the glow of the TV
punching
the over starched sheets
in your pay-by-the-week
hotel room.

Nothing left
but another empty
ass-pocket
of 3 dollar Heaven Hill
telling you to go
& get more.

Nothing left
but candy wrappers,
empty Chinese food boxes,
& coke cans,
that litter the counters
& floors
like lonely corpses
upon a battle field.

Nothing left
but your soon to be ex-wife
occasionally coming back

to fuck you,
giving you false hope
of reconciliation,
but she only rides you
on the cheap blue carpet
to get you to sign
the divorce papers.

Nothing left
but that one stupid idea,
going to Visions strip club
with the 50 bucks
that you borrowed,
thinking it would solve
all the agony ripping inside
of your stomach.

Nothing left
but the shower you take,
the scars that you soap,
& the dirty shirt
you stick in the dryer,
in the hopes that
no one can smell
last night's liquor
all over your body.

Nothing left
but 50 cent Dixie cup beers
at the strip club,
each one a mouthful
of warm spit & foam,
but you drink them anyway,
wanting to save just enough money
so a cheap perfumed pussy
will rub itself

onto your thigh.

Nothing left
but the defeated
& drunk 3 mile
walk back to the hotel
with only 5 dollars left
for those fast burning
cigarettes
& a few tacos.

Nothing left
but the cars that zip by you
as you walk along the highway,
& they're filled with happy families,
& you imagine
your family inside one
of them,
happy just being together,
kissing your wife
& teasing your child.

Nothing left
but the street lights
lighting up small parts
of vacant concrete.

Nothing left
but walking faster
towards that one spot,
wanting to use it
as a source of energy
to jump start
your heart.

Nothing left

but the sex on the other side
of the paper-thin
hotel walls
making you envious
& jealous.

Nothing left
but thinking of a late night woman
you can call
so you can match
the orgasms
you're forced to listen to.

Nothing left
but wanting to join
the crack-heads
walking like zombies
outside your window.

Nothing left
but the small table
you sit at
in your hotel room.

Nothing left
but the realization
of total isolation.

Nothing left
but the poems
you should be
writing.

The Little Toy

you rubbed
the little plastic tyrannosaurus goodbye,
told me to take him,
& when i returned i could give
him back to you.

you said that his teeth
were sharp,
& he would protect me
if i ever got lonely
or scared.

your little pudgy hands
reached up
across the sun.
your hair,
        a fire's blonde,
traced the outer edges
of the little toy.

you said again, it's okay...take him.

with your surviving eyes
that were not much
different
than
mine,
you convinced me.

& all these years later,
his teeth
are still sharp,
        he has not lost
any

color,

& he's been to every reading,
been in every poem,
ripping, biting, protecting.

i've tried
to drink him away,
womanize him away.

i've tried
to ignore him,
deny him,
& live without him, but

he claws his way through the bag
that he still sits in
& howls with a vicious roar.

it's been 7 years,
& he's still doing all he can
to get
back to where
he
belongs.

Even the Virgin Mary Packed Her Suitcase

sometimes there's a hole
so deep
that you have
no choice but
to acknowledge
what others refuse
                    to see.

As You Were...

"Well, Francis,
it has been a year
& the identities are finally
coming together.
You've worked so hard.
I'm so proud of you!"

I got up & left after
the session was over.
I took the usual route home
across the highway,
through the park,
& into the streets near my
house,
& as I hit the alleyway,
I saw a budding flower
in the middle of a bunch
of dead ones. I thought:

How good is looking
at a beautiful flower,
or a blue sky,
without several different
opinions?

How good is feeling
reborn
without the laughter
of the unseen man
ashing his cigar
on my head?

How good is a new toy
without the joyous approval

of the little boy?

How good is meditation
without
the rebellious priest
breathing for me?

How good is a football game
without the town drunk
screaming for me?

How much fun
can the poem be when
the agitator
has vanished into the skies
with all of the other
ignorant birds?

How enjoyable can buying
anything be
when the hustler
is not there with his
bargaining skills?

My little group
of silent assassins
(who had protected me
all of these years,
who had let me check out
while they dealt with
all of the agony,
love, & torment,
while I was off somewhere
living in photographs)
are all but gone now.

& as I stood by myself
looking at the one flower
in the middle
of all the dead ones,

I felt the terrible sting
of loneliness,
as if I had just lost cherished
friends & family members.

& when my eyes began
to water,
& my heart began
to break into shards,
I asked myself:

Is it because of loss,
or is it because
I had never
seen this kind
of glowing red
in a flower before?

The Morning After

when i came to,
i was at the bottom
of the stairs
in the park.

my face was
a beaten pulp
of bloody teeth
& cut lips.

i had no memory
of why or how
i ended up
at the bottom
of the stairs
at dawn, but
i could hear
the morning birds,
& i could see
dogs running free
without
their leashes.

they ignored their
master's calls,
tongues dangling
over their
jaws, ears
held up by
the speeds
of the wind.

after i pulled myself

up off the ground,
everything hurt;
my back,
my legs,
my head,
& my neck.

i limped over
to a bench,
sat down, & tried
to remember.

i tried to think,
but after a certain
moment,
after a certain
point in time,
everything
eventually goes
black.

i lit a cigarette
& sat my flesh
back into the bench,
watching everything
but nothing.

i saw a man
not far off playing
his guitar,
his head was down,
his fingers
moved up & down
the fretboard with ease.

nothing mattered,

& it sounded
like a concert,
like having sex
during a hurricane
while the city
was being evacuated.

no one else
was around.

it felt like he was playing
for only me,
& when i looked
at the distance
it would take me
to walk
back to my room,
he began to play
faster & faster,
his fingers like gods
tickling the rosebuds
hidden deeply within
my soul.

it was more
than i dared
to think
about.

Tomb

even if it be as cold
as a tomb,
 i shall continue to walk
these paths
without a face.

Outside

The park animals
play in the trees
like 100 marvelous
naked women
cartwheeling
throughout the grass.

Two Oak Geisha

two oak geisha, gently silhouetted
by the midnight lamp of the moon,

one, twisting and turning the shadows
through the thinness of her arches,

the other, glowing
as undressed ladies often do.

Follow it

within the quiet mind
of every man,
is a snow capped
mountain range,
patiently waiting
to avalanche
into the folds
of discourse & memory.

"Why is that guy looking up?"

if the tips of the tall pines continue
to paint the sky in that way,
my veins will become an easel,
my heart, a multicolored palette.

If I could just be

a simple ray of light
exposing
the morning flowers, or

a fierce blast of wind
pushing snow across
the mountain tops,

then I'd never need
to write again.

The Singing Heart

i dip the green tea bag
up & down
in the hot water

& much like
my singing heart

it quickly adapts
to the void

 by coloring the water
silently.

While Lacing Up My Hiking Boots

i noticed the young poet posturing
& blowing kisses into the mirror.

he must be stressing about his image again,
i thought, while fastening my pack,

but when he began tapping his foot
& looking obsessively at his wristwatch,

i knew right away that he was dying to announce
the publication of yet another one of his poems.

Gathering Up My Gear

The young poet asked:
why don't you attend writer's retreats
& conferences with other writers?

I responded: my pack, my hiking boots,
my compass, & my walking stick
are the only group of writers I'll ever need
to be around.

But don't you want their input
& their criticism? he asked.

Gathering up my gear for another hike, I replied:
with each step & with each breath,
the wild, mountains, trees, plants & trails
supply me with all the criticism that I need.

The Deal

i love knowing
that it has finally
gotten to the point
where each poem
is forgotten
after it has been
written.

Skip James on the Radio

like palm to face,
foot to dirt,
whip to back,
eye to mirror,
fist to door,
shoulder to rage, and
mind to past,

denial
is a strong liquor, and
like all strong liquors,
it will consume you
before it can
wear off.

Bone Song

the maggots will feast
on my bones
with compassion;
a fitting time to write.

Lightness

"Paradise!" Basho yelled
into lightness of empty wine jug;
the poem had only begun.

Blood Music

every bird feather
that I find & stick
in my hat
is a love poem
dedicated
to all those anxiety
fueled days
& nights
that I was trapped
in a chair
or the back seat
of a car
with no means
of escape
other than
rocking myself
back & forth
to the music
of my very own blood.

All the Jazz You'll Need

Squirrel sits on humble broken limb
playing his acorn
like Coltrane's saxophone.
O' Bodhisattva!

It's Fine, Really

sitting in the woods
with Japhy Ryder's Turtle Island;
enlightened squirrel flips me off.

CHAINSAW

for months
dead flowers sit on mantle;
who's fooling who?

Fire in the Fingertips

I sit on a park bench
& dream of long red hair
in photographs,

how it wraps around
milk-white shoulders
only to mesmerize
like American wile,

how it flaunts itself
along the curves
of bottomless desolation
where there are no meanings
nor perceptions,

& only out of habit
is there even a belief
in the images
we've seeded
from within,

for there are no awakened ones;
only simple truths
that we position
beyond our reach.

80 Rolls

i no longer need
to take photographs
because the poems
are now taking
photographs of me.

You Think It's Easy?

Yesterday,
the angry hobo,
with his bottles of wine
& two old suitcases,
walked into my house
& made himself
comfortable.

"I told you
I'd find you," he said,
while putting his feet up
on my writing table.

"You think all this
hiking, writing,
& meditation
is going to save you?
I've been taking
it easy on you, son,
letting you think
you've got the upper
hand...well, I'm only
getting warmed up!"

As I sat there
unable to speak,
drunk, half hung-over,
& without mind
or vision,
the angry hobo
grinned the grins
of heavyweight champs,
lit my cigar,

& said, "Now, I'm going
to go fuck
your girlfriend."

The Bandit

While men are too busy
seeking gods
inside houses built
for the killin',
I'm under the watchful eyes
of the squirrels & birds;
carving the word 'truth'
into every single fallen log
that the woods has provided.

Some Say We Should Always Have Goals

but
I'm
nothing
more
than
a desolate
traveler
who's
walking
through
the
hours
of
your
life.

Two Panic Attacks Before 10 a.m.

as the distorted view
of my hand
continues to evolve
within the stem
of the wineglass,
i shall grow more
& more fond
of these obsessions
that cause me
such great pain.

Until the Scotch is Gone

she said,"i like the way
you sing
songs."

i said that i
did not sing
any songs.

"exactly," she said,
putting her hand
up my thigh.

Roll Around Your Couch Like A Hurricane

she said,
you are not a good artist.
you don't promote
self awareness or change.

i was lying down
on one side of the couch
& i rolled over to the
other side,

are you happy?

Tiki Statue

when you
need their
love &
accolades,
it's apparent
that your art
has abandoned
you.

The Killing Grounds

in a world full
of aging
bone-yards,
O, how
obvious
we must
be.

One Hour Per Cup

no matter how foolish
human nature
may seem,

drunk & loud
under
the judgment
of stars,

it will all come back
to tea,
eventually.

All the Tight Little Asses in the Universe

the bar owner's son
fills out
the following week's
work schedule

& he asks everyone
what days
they can & cannot
work, & he's
pretty accommodating
about it all, but

he gives Jenny
whatever days she
wants.

at first i thought
it was her
blonde hair &
tight little ass,

until i was walking
to the bathroom
and saw them hugging
over by the
supply closet,
her hands on his crotch,
his hands
on her tight ass.

you'd never expect
a young woman like
her to go for a guy
with the wavy

thick hair,

breath like an
old onion, and
a gut like a large
bag of taco
meat, but

when he pulled out
his wad of money
& i saw
his aging
& alcoholic
father,

i knew at an instant,
that tight little
blonde asses

will have
their motives
too.

Never Understood

we are all clowns
dancing
in love;
so why not?

PTSD

Programmed
to
suffer
delusions

Not Until the Symphony Ends

sitting here listening to Mahler's Resurrection,
with the Christmas lights
still strung up around my apartment
from the year before,
i think of you;

all those whiskey soaked times
when we'd eat once a day,
(sometimes less)
when we walked to the bars
& drank at 11 in the morning,
played pool,
& pretended that our hearts
were big huge windmills
blowing across Five Points.

those were the days you'd walk out on me,
& you'd do it every other day,
with an angry click-clack from your high heels,
& the last thing that i always saw
was your big ass trying to fit through
the crack of our broken door.

i liked that big ass of yours,
how it felt in my hand
when i grabbed it firmly, but
you had too much life in you
to take notice, so much life in fact,
that while i was grabbing it,
& pushing your body into mine,
you'd ignore me, grab the bottle
from my other hand,
& drink straight from it
until i let go.

those days, those hungry days
when death was ready to take us both,
when my pants needed a new belt,
when you no longer fit into your bra,
those were the days when i began to write more,

when i'd feel death's cold skeletal gaze
over my shoulder, whispering
"you think this will save you?"
& i'd want to quit, but you'd open a beer,
walk it over to me with massive hips swaying,
& place it next to my computer.
it was always just enough to send death
to the next house,
where the man doing his taxes fell dead,
or where the man cutting his lawn
dropped cold in the middle of the summer heat.

then, one day, you were gone.
you packed it in, had enough of surviving,
said you were headed for the coast,
or maybe Muscle Shoals.

i sometimes wonder if you made it there,
& i wonder if your clicking high heels
are driving some other poor soul into fits of rage,
or maybe you gave up all together,
became a mother, or a campaign speech writer.

i never gave up. i'm still here
sharing a cup of tea with death
as he checks his watch
& taps his foot impatiently upon my floor.

it has always been that way for me

& all that it ever needs to be;
a way & means of keeping the gorillas
secure in the cages of my mind,

but when it's not enough,
i do have these Christmas lights
& sometimes i need them in May or June,
but now, i need them more than ever.

onto the next

too many days
spent drunk
& not enough
of them spent
chopping logs
& whittling
them down
into walking sticks
where the muscles
of my shoulders
& chest meet
to drip sweat
onto a trail
created
by the slightest
glimpse of light
trapped between
the sole of a boot
& the poked holes
of a well soiled earth.

Harvest, Alabama

after i watched them speak
in tongues,

after they rattled off
dance moves
up & down
the velvet aisles
of the damned,

after they put
their hands on my head
& prayed the prayers
of the guilty,

& after they placed "sacred" oils
on my tattoos
& chanted for my soul
while i laughed
the laugh of the doomed,

i walked out of the church
& thought:

the chimps have taken
over the ship's controls!

& they're headed straight
for the iceberg
with such an immense hatred
in their eyes

that even the birds
of beauty
have given up

& lost every last bit
of their worm-filled
innards!

if by ash, or by grass

like a fist full
of flowers,

& like tits
heaving from a corset,

the urns of hell
will soon
have their way.

Realizing Patagonia

i awoke this morning
as a tea leaf,

where a Ruan song
was in place
of a long
& passive yawn,

the sound, well-centered
& content
to be the lining
of my veins,

& much like
the lake sky
of Maine
in summertime,

(where i had once fallen
in love
with the broken rocks
under my hiking
boots)

there were no longer
multiple thoughts
coming to multiple conclusions,

in fact,
there was only
one thought left,

one hot kettle
filled by only water,

& the water poured onto
& infused out
the many illusions
of the self
& of the past,

leaving nothing
to ponder over,
other than,

was i finally ready
to be tasted?

i must've been,

for i just took
the first step
towards realizing
Patagonia.

For Lilly

every bus ride
in between
effort
& effortless,

every beer
in between
black out
& sleep
deprivation,

every face seen
in between
stranger
& random acts
of kindness,

every mirror
in between
shattered by
hand
& the truth seen
within the glow
of a vacancy
sign,

every card sent
in between
an empty wallet
& a crisp 20
for a new baby doll,

every phone call

to the lawyer
in between
the 'good luck'
& the hang up,

every break down
in between
the agony
of endless tears
& the dancing
shadow boxer
by the midnight moon
at 2 a.m.;

in between them all
lives a feeling
casting an equal, but
indifferent shadow
over every night
& every day, but

on the other side,
there can
only exist a hug,

a hug
that wraps around
my waist,

& due to your
height,

it holds my guts
in place
for the first time
in my life.

6 Days on the Crescent Line

& the
thunderin'
wheels
of
the
train
said:
the
interesting
thing
about
a roaming
heart
is
that
it doesn't
need
any
brakes
when
fiery
sparks
are
kissing
steel
before
the
switch.

The Greatest Poetry Reading of All Time

happened on a new fall afternoon
as i stood behind
a group of pine trees
watching two rival groups
of Canadian geese.

they flapped their wings
& stood up in the river,
honking loud verse
with breasts pushed forward.

& when one finished,
the others would chase him away
by ripping out
some of his feathers,

leaving only a small trail
of his former self,
his former words,
that floated on smooth waters
like a fog of icy wine.

Somewhere Underneath Spain

in plain & readable language
the worms are busy
conveying
the sorrow of Lorca's
shallow grave
to the twisting
roots
of the juniper
trees.

Uncle Leo's Cloud of Smoke

at my grandfather's wake,
Uncle Leo & i
smoked cigarettes
together
in the Croswell Funeral Home
basement,

Leo's face;drawn out,
blank,quiet
& listless
as he inhaled
Lucky Strike
after Lucky Strike
into his bony
&narrow face,

Leo must've smoked
15 non filtered
cigarettes
to every one of mine,

& it did not phase him,
in fact,he never once
coughed,or uttered
a single word to me,

until,i asked,
"Uncle Leo,
what was my grandfather
like when he was younger?"

Leo leaned forward
from the chair,

& let the slits
of his blue eyes
cut through
the smoke cloud,

"he was the toughest
son-of-a-bitch
i ever knew!" he shouted
"there was not one
person
who could've out drank,
out worked,
out punched,
or out lived Francis!"

& as quickly as he
appeared
to me,
he once again
vanished,

back to his
safe&secure cloud
of smoke,

where each one
of his inhales
sent him
back to his youth
so he could have
at least
one more beer
with his brothers
in South Boston
&Dorchester,

&his cloud of smoke
continued to grow
bigger
&bigger
around our heads,

because,
he had to keep
lighting
more&more
cigarettes,

because,
with each exhale
came the agonizing
reminder
that he was truly
the last one
left.

A Letter to Father Costigan

truth is,
i don't enjoy
the world
very much
when i'm sober,

i've spent months
upon
months,trying

to convince
myself
that i can enjoy life
without
hard liquor,

& i come up
with some dull activities
like bird watching,
meditation,
sitting in parks,
& watching films,
but

after awhile
i'm left completely
bored
with the world,

bored with
the sound
of my own
bullshit

voice,

bored with
the shrink's
pretentious
advice,

bored with
former drunks
telling me
their personal
survival
stories,

bored with
the pills
the doctors
have given me
to help calm
the mental side
of sobriety.

truth is,
i like the way
the soul
of my elbow
feels
when leaning into
the dark oak
of the bar,

i'm elated
with the sudden jolt
of confidence
that travels down
my spine

after ordering
a 'Jameson neat',

& that first sip,
that first real burn
that falls down
my throat,
is just like liquid gold

& it feels better than
art,sex,power,
war
& money combined,

truth is,
i love bars,
i love the stench
of them.

i love the dark
private corners,
the smelly
bathrooms,
& the bartender's
shitty stories,

i enjoy the crappy
cover bands
that play god awful
renditions
of CCR songs

& it fills me with happiness
to watch
middle aged
drunk people

dance around
to 'Fortunate Son',

truth is,
i feel at home
in bars,

it feels normal
& very much
like family,

i enjoy people's
elated
& lonely
facial expressions,

the sway of a woman's
body
as she looks
for a good place
to sit,

the loud&drunk
quarrels
between
jealous lovers,

it fills me with joy
&excitement
when a fight
breaks out,

truth is,
i love it all;
the glossy eyes,
the slurring speech,

the drunk asshole
who thinks
he's a hot shot

& the liars who tell
you
that they are
connected
to mobsters.

then,there are those
who'll say
"you could die
of a heart attack
if you drink too much"

"you could get
diabetes,cancer
or lose all of your teeth"

"you could end up in jail,
or even worse;
all alone!"

it's true,all of those things
could happen,
& a few of them
have happened
to me,but

i could also get hit
by a truck
on my way
to the store,

or even worse,

stub my toe
on a chair
while trying to find
the bathroom
in the middle
of the night.

one time,
right after catholic mass,
a priest told me
"god gives everyone
at least one special talent",

well,Father Costigan,
after 38 years of travel,
trial
& error,
i've discovered
that I'm very good
at sitting
inside of bars
& drinking hard liquor,

because,
truth is,
the world
is just a very
boring place
without them.

A Conversation

"what do you have
going on
next week?"

"I have
a job interview"

"for what?"

"a mechanic's job,
minor car repairs
for a rental company;
fixing breaks,
oil changes,
tire repair etc."

"i thought
your poetry
collections
supported you?"

"no, not even
the dead
masters could
support
themselves
with poetry
collections"

"then, how
did they become
masters?"

"respect,

they earned a name;
they were hard
workers,but
they also had
to have jobs
to support
the writing"

"I've read a lot
of John Grisham
&he's loaded!"

"if you want
to write
genre fiction
&get a movie
deal
that's different"

"is that why
women
have always
left you,
because
you never had
any real money?"

"probably"

"ever since you
were little
you always
did things
the hard way,
your way, why?"

"because
it feels quite
like nothing else
in the world
when you actually
succeed"

"like publishing
a book?"

"just like publishing
a book"

"I just don't get it,
you could go back
to school
&get a real career,
seems like a waste
of time
when you could
be making
the real bucks"

"what's wrong
with fixing cars?"

"nothing is wrong
with fixing cars,
if you like
being someone's
bitch"

"&college will
free me of that?"

"it will give you a better

shot at being free"

"i'm already
free"

"what about retirement,
what will you
have when you retire?"

"not much"

"don't you want retirement,
a big house,
and a few cars?"

"I never had that stuff,
so I probably
wouldn't know what
to do with it
if I did"

"future, you never think
about your future,
you're just chasing
a ghost
with all this writing stuff
if you ask me"

"i did not ask you"

"you should have
asked me,
you could have been
a priest, or a lawyer"

"like John Grisham?"

"yes, he's a lawyer in real life
at least when you fail
you'd have a good job
to fall back on"

"I fail everyday
at the keyboard"

"then why do
you waste
so much time with it?"

"so I can repair
other people's cars"

University Drive

It really is something to look out the window
of your studio apartment
at 3 a.m.
while University Drive
is still empty,

it feels like sneaking whiskey into
The Old Towne Coffee Shop
or like the first time a woman
ever walked naked
towards the bottom of your bed.

There's no hate in the bones,
just the quiets
of cigarette smoke,
the silent stack of books with broken
spines
&the dirty forks that are happy to be left
untouched in the sink.

Yes,there's nothing quite like
being alone,
sitting in boxer shorts
in front of the dark window
with a full ashtray
&nothing really happening,

it's very different from the daytime
when angry neighbors
bang on the floors
about the music level,

or the pissed off women who call

every 15 minutes
so you can give them updates
about what you're doing
&not doing,but

pretty soon there will be a bunch
of people
driving up&down University
with their cars, loud music
&hateful protest,

on their way to work,
or on their way to buy expensive caffeine drinks
or on their way to forgetting about
what put them there in the first place,

&it leaves me sad knowing
that they'll never even think
about looking out of a window
at the magic happening
on University
at 3 a.m.,

but, it also fills me with joy knowing
that my little secret
is probably known by only
5 other people
in a city full of thousands,

&how exciting a secret can be
when it's one simple thing,
but feels like one million gems
continuously
falling from the heart
&hitting the floor
with an unstoppable force.

#2

today i sat
inside Saint Leo's
Catholic church;

mostly
for the silence,
mostly
for the stained glass;

when a little old priest
with a limp
&one good eye
sat next to me

"i'm not going to attempt
any discussion,
nor do i have the time
to philosophize"
he said
while leaning back
into the pew,

and there it was...

the ravens of the damned

always make art out
of the mundane,
always use the dull skull
of death
as a carnation upon your lapel
so the people of the world
will smell it
&be left in total ecstasy,
always create, until,
there are no waltzes left in you,
or, until,
the ravens of the damned
can no longer circle
your head
like millions of uneasy
tiny black shards
screaming in agony.

The Last Time I Saw You

we were sitting together
in the corner booth
next to the big window
of the Kaffeeklatsch

we drank Yuenglings,
&talked about moving
to Kansas City together
&how the stars seemed
lazy that night,

&while I went on&on
about the silent people
outside the big window,
you rubbed your beer bottle
against mine

&even though we had screwed
a few hours earlier,
it was your way, the only way,
you could rub something of yours
up against mine,

I remember your tight dark Levis
that night
&how they captured your thighs,
how the small bell at the bottom
exposed a tiny bit
of your deep black boots,

you looked good, too good
for the last goodbye
before I hopped on the Greyhound

to Kansas City.

It's during the awkward moments
when people begin to pretend,
instead,
of saying goodbye,

they make grand plans
rather than saying
"it's all over now"

they talk about spending warm
California days together,
adventures
into New Mexico,
&creating art in Colorado,

&they'll go on&on
creating their fake worlds
&making their fake plans
for moments
that will never take place.

In truth,
you were too scared to say it,
your friends hated me
because I was poor
&opinionated,

your mom hated me
because she was a baptist
&I was the heathen
who made her daughter
scream in perfect rhythm
with the bounce
of the headboard,

but, there we were,
two people
trying to make a fire
by rubbing ice cubes
together,

unable to move the chess pieces
of the damned
into checkmate
&call it quits,

"I'll be in Kansas City in
a few months"
you said

&as I grabbed your fat ass
one last time
I told you that I would wait
for you.

when I left with my suitcase
I watched you
from outside the big window,
your finger slowly tapped
against the beer bottle,

you could no longer see me,
I had become one
of the silent people
outside the window,

just another guy with all
of his belongings
in a suitcase,

just another guy
who let the moon swallow
him whole
as he walked towards
the bus depot.

Nowadays I hear you live
with a much younger guy,

that you're full of anxieties
&you never leave
your apartment,

I hear you've abandoned
your friends,
&moved somewhere else,

imagine that!

Today the news is talking
about a possible war
with North Korea,

some kind
of "missile crisis",
that the North Koreans could
bomb us
at any moment,

I just don't give a shit
anymore.

Confetti

standing at the busy crosswalk
of South Broadway
I think:

if only I had the courage
to walk out
in front of these trucks,

it would only take one
step,
one magnificent leap
of courage.

the drivers would come
to a screeching stop
terrified, but curious,

the people
looking out their busy
work windows
would hold their hands
over gasping mouths

&not because my lungs,
limbs
&bones are all over
the road,

but, because,

I instantly popped
&vanished
like a child's balloon

leaving no trace
of myself,
other than,

a steady drift
of multi-colored
confetti,

slowly raining down
upon
the horrors
of their average
everyday
mundane lives.

as i light another cigarette

the shadow
breathes
behind
the crucifix

The Washington Avenue Bridge

I began to obsessively rub
my grandmother's old rosary beads
together
as the #16 bus started to drive over
the Washington Avenue Bridge,

the same bridge, where years earlier,
John Allyn Smith
with enormous sparrow wings
cried out for 'Henry'
from the rails of his gut
while plummeting
into eternal laughter,

&I was still methodically rubbing
them together
when the bus reached
the other side of the bridge,
but, like most things that are held
onto for too long,
the string finally snapped
&the beads fell
like bullets without owners
into the ongoing darkness
of my vacant jacket pocket.

Reaching Fuchsia

i was alone in the middle
of the Badlands
at 7 a.m.
with my little radio
sitting upon
the tiny clay butte.

it had felt like ages,
getting myself up
to where the sky
touched
rugged landscapes,

but with full red beard
& boots dusted grey
with rock, climb,
& skill,
i played the music
i had hidden
in my wind breaker's
front pocket.

the sounds moved the land
around me
in swirls of incomplete,
but solved puzzles,
sounds that would soon
fall into
blossom,

sounds for the bison to roam
through the grasslands,
for the hawk

to dip & dive among the cliffs,
for the prairie dog
to pop up
& down
from his hole.

my legs instantly grew
11 feet in length,
my arms,
like long torches,
painted the pinks
& yellows
hidden
within the clouds.

i was one note away,
one scream
into the massive widths
of the barrens,
from escaping
the distant eyes
of my humanness.

it was complete freedom,
it was fuchsia
colored sparklers
inside my ribs
burning down
the locked doors
of the chest's
stubborn flesh.

Momentary Loss of Freedom

looking everywhere
to gratify the senses

is to suffer, a

removal of
perfect catatonic,

confusing bright
& dark
with mind's voice,

contaminating

the empty flowers
within the bones
of nothingness

with the mouthy
gunshots
of humanness.

father to son

the rambler,
fit to kill,

dirty jeans
& muscle
legs,

forever watched
by your heart

turning
over & over

inside
the hubcaps
of every
18 wheeler
the sun had
enough
courage
to shine upon
that day.

Packed,
unpacked,

moving forward
& in reverse,

hitting
the north
& south bound
corridors

of the Mason/Dixon
line,

right after

you had run out
on any
woman

whose name
happened
to sound like
it ended
in Y.

Sought religion,

found it
in the gospels
according
to Mom & Pop's
hotel diner,

where you ordered
short stacks,
orange juice,
bacon,
& extra syrup

from the impatient
& fish-netted thighs
of all-night waitresses

who chewed on gum
like they
chewed on men.

You hung
your washed clothes
above the sink

or used them
as cum
catchers

to capture
the loud
& lonely moans
of Susan,
or Sally Mae.

You drank
them up
afterwards

&laughed
them out, but

not before
you stole
what was
left over

&turned them
into
the rhythm
& blues.

Nevada,
Texas,
& Vermont,

it's all the same,

except for
the sounds
of the pavement

& the star-struck
eyes
of the road kill,

but when your nose
connected
with the foul smell
for the first time,

your head jerked
with disgust;

just like an old
dog
unable to stand
his
own howl,

& just like the father
who taught
his son
the ways
of the pariah
at age 9.

& it quickly becomes
you,

& you, it,

forever trapped
by it,

& forever driving
upon it;

the long road
built
by your
finest bullshit

& your dirtiest
broken promises.

Running Out on Nashville

Nashville at night from bus terminal
understands living, its heartless youth
made from young girls' blush.
Loud eyes on uppers & coffee, searching for the fire
from wood-chipped sleeping benches.
Hands full of quietness, they wonder
who's Laredo, who's Pittsburgh, who's St. Louis?

Bus driver chews on souls & spits indifference.
Most of us have had enough of dying before breeding,
so said the man cleaning the windows,
so said the ticket counter girls & the cowboy
dancing for Fort Worth. The shirts are 3 days dirty.
The hands have been down the pants of John Wesley Hardin.

Line up, hand over those tickets, find your seats quickly!
I got a window seat next to a jelly-bellied Samoan. He smells.
Nashville at 2 a.m., with your avenues of preachers
& "goodwill" toward armies of under-bridge drunks,
I hate you! I'd rather be anywhere, even midnight in Mogadishu.
The diesel pedal pumps.
I've never heard of sleep before.

For **Bill Taylor Jr.**

Every sidewalk holds a pulsating silence, alone.
After many hours of stillness, cold beer,
& in my head: the death of Stuart Perkoff.
He's not in it, or here, finally.
It's true we can stand around too much, but
who needs the structured views of architecture?
Blood's crucifix is heavy enough on its own.
& from behind the prison girls,
Bill & I stand like shores of leveled eyelids,
in tune with click-clacking pavement,
unmoved & content to be cornered in by the incidents.
From the cooler we pick out two of the coldest beers,
the muse:
teaching us a thing or two about 3 in the afternoon.

Custom Built

before Death
can point
his
South
Boston,
custom built,
sawed-off
shot gun
at you,
make sure
he knows
just how
drunk
with life
the rose
hanging
out of
your
mouth is
as you
spin
your
bones
to the
music
of your
choice

Let it Burn

he had always felt
that the fire knew
too much about him,

but he'd sit
in front
of it anyway.

when he fed it
more leaves
& twigs,

he'd stare directly
into its hellish heat
of reds & oranges

until it engulfed
every last part
of his face,

until the screaming
rage coming from the cold
finally went silent,

until it melted
the proud veins
that had once pumped

throughout
his entire
body.

Chablis

she drinks boxed white wine
until 5 a.m.,
no one around,
the world quiet,
the husband snoring on
the couch.

it's how she likes it,
her bones
settled inside
her private bubble.

& if there is one sound,
one movement,
that slinks its way
through the darkness
& scares her,

she'll raise the glass,
(glowing full of Chablis
with the soft
light of her computer
screen) press her eye
against it,

& look through it
like a telescope,

the world,
colorful, easy, & still.

Blowtorch

this path, alone,
kills a mother's
neglect,

it laughs
at the poet
who seeks
redemption,

it grins at the
aging drill Sargent
with his old
polished
medals
& worn out
war stories,

this path, alone,
dines on
the present
time at hand
& pisses out
the whining
apparitions,

it feeds lonely
& hungry animals
while ignoring
the diabetic nation,

this path,
this small wooded,
& natural path,
the last

thing alive,

the last thing
standing,

will blowtorch
every last bit
of the world's
foolish
ideologies,

smile
the smiles
of kings,
& never look
back.

One in the Pocket

my little pocket notebook
that I scribble secret poems into
while I sit alone
in the fresh air of the woods,
is much like a little Buddha
planting flowers
in the void.

Good Song

I'm here,
drinking the wine
of good song,

living in a world
created
for myself,

where illusions
touch the bottom
of clarity,

where the sons
& daughters
of Junior Kimbrough
bring emptiness
to rock-torn
bottoms,

where boundless
transformations
of body, harmony,
& battlefield
balance,

& the good songs
go on, simple
as a child's picture

in hand, pencil
cloaked in patio
sunlight

& silence lingers,

on top before
it vanishes
into a thousand
places I ignored.

"you're not real,
you're not bone,
madness, or truth,
you don't write
about the streets"

"you don't write
of the common man, or
you don't have
the training, or
academic prowess
to even be writing"

i've heard it
all before, and
i've heard

that's it's good
to wipe up
and not down, and

i've heard
that's it's good
for the magician
to hide
the rabbit
before the trick
is exposed,

the thing
about good song

is that there
is no way
to pretend it,

it's a flower-path
mountain
without mercy,

it's the immortal
beer in the hands
of a big breasted
woman,

it's the hello
and the farewell
of a wordless
monk,

it's nobody,
it's me, it's kindling
for the fire.

Dig In

as i pull back the skin of the fruit
in order to get to the pulp
& juicy center,
i am filled with joy just knowing
that i've had it wrong all this time.

The Craftsmen

after all the music
within my blood
is said & done,

at least there will be
an original corpse
so silent
& wonderful

that the people
will have no choice
but to finally
leave their flowers.

hallway

inside the cross,
inside the lotus,
inside the prayer bead,
inside the breath
&inside the atheist

there's nothing
for the weary,

no corners to hide in,
no drawers
full of old photo albums,

just a long
eternal hallway

where revenge
against
the mind
is unattainable.

10

"i see you're going out
into the woods, once again,
where i am sure you'll fall in love
with trees, animals, & fresh air!"

"no doubt, baby,
with fuckin' hiking boots blazin'!"

"what's your dumb fascination
with those old ugly ass boots?"

"unless you've stomped
on the iron hearts of empires
with every step taken,
you'd never understand!"

Flush the Dream Until You Laugh

as he picked up the dead flowers
from the vase, the petals
fell off and the stems
crumbled
into his hands, but

this did not make him sad,
because
he remembered
how the flowers
brightened up his parlor
for days and days.

he thanked them for this
as he walked to
the trash barrel
to throw them away.

when the dead flowers
finally vanished into the void
of the plastic garbage bag,
he burst into
uncontrollable
laughter.

"damn," he shouted, with his fists
high up in the air,
"only in the hearts of men
do you find the desire
to live forever."

To Hike a Painted Canyon

I

Among the roots, trees, boulders, and minerals, I ask these questions:

What odd voice, like rain, will challenge oblivion,
whether joined by a softened silence equal to my bones,
or by the falcon's wingspan that fades into complacency
over the ever changing faces of the earth?

What walk, what hike, what climb of mortal splendor
will pull the ripeness out from an insufferable master's
desolate thought?

And if autumn diminishes her mossy temper before leaves fall,
will man's immense heavy wants, needs, and suffering
cross from the veins of their mother's wombs
and melt into cycles of listless compost?

I ask these questions, like secret little things ask the trees,
in silence, in the heart left over to sighs, in the arteries of cocooning
plant life hanging over the edges of the dirt.
I want this gnaw to avenge the triumph on my face
and leave it heavy necked among the ladies with their bark thighs,
but the trace thoughts in my brain are split in two,
like the wolf left to decide while roaming among the dead in the
battlefield.

II

Trails begin with the mistaken, the hurt ones, the drunk ones,
the ones who are sick of life, the beaten down,
the ones who arrive at the very last door full of ideologies.
There is a bone fear so dark that the first step will take a

silent form, that form will take the left-over parts of the gods,
stitch them together, and create disillusionment,

but the wild rabbit, the wild hawk, the wild boar need not
shrill nor undress themselves at the feet of fearful agony,
for their temperance waits in the cold, ready to live loudly,
passionately, beautifully, to strike, to gather strength
and burrow their muscle into groans of pleasure.

III

And if it be by walking stick, pack, and patience
that I grow too tired and too mad to continue on
these paths of instant glory,
only all the better,
for the boulders will wait for me to sit,
the trees will wait for me to lean,
the rivers will wait for me to clean, and cook,
the dome of stars above will become my blanket,
and the grassy earth will be my mattress.

When I do stop, stretch out, or sit in lotus,
the air, much like the pleasant smile before the first
sip of ale, will hold me in her living silence and void me
of all compulsions.
She'll show me her picturesque mountains,
speak to me through the language of the flowers.
She'll bring my tissues and blood together with blustery winds,
pull out the black tar rage with reflections inside the pond.

IV

Humanity will completely vanish while walking consciously among
nature, and the heart, like the sun breaking through the dark spots

among the trees, will find itself opening and weaving through
webs of air.
It will wander in the directions of the wind, infinitely searching,
but infinitely full of joy:

O trees! O rocks! O rivers! O mountains!
O buttes! O animals! O ferns! O natural music!
I hold your teachings deep within my fibers,
deep within my blood that no longer needs to cough!
I sing your songs exploding from my wide-set shoulders,
O wild, how you ripped out my ego
with your greens, purples, reds, browns, and oranges!

Goodbye, heavy burdens of agony!
Goodbye, derision! Goodbye, apathy!
Goodbye, hangovers! Goodbye, ghosts that lingered!
Goodbye, heavy guilt! Goodbye, voices of mother and father!
Goodbye, money! Goodbye, useless jobs!
Goodbye, suffering! Goodbye, my old masters!

O, the world is finally beautiful,
colorful, and dancing
with her paints!

Alive! Alive! Alive! At last!

A finish here...

188

Frank Reardon was born in 1974, in Boston, MA and spent his first 28 years living there. Since then, he has lived all over the country in places such as Alabama, Kansas City and Rhode Island. He currently resides in the Badlands of North Dakota, still looking for a way to get out. Frank has been published in various reviews, journals and online literary zines. His first book, *Interstate Chokehold,* was published by NeoPoiesis Press in 2009. His second book, *Nirvana Haymaker,* was published by NeoPoiesis in 2012.

More about Frank Reardon and 'Blood Music' –

"Read Frank Reardon at your own risk. He'll open your heart with a corkscrew and leave you wide-eyed and longing for more."

—Dan Fante, author of *Chump Change, Mooch,"86'd"* and *Spitting Off Tall Buildings*

"Like the sound of blood thrumming through veins during a life defining moment, so is the importance of Frank Reardon's writing in *Blood Music*. His writing will make you feel as if your heart is in a vice or expanding transcendentally during moments of bliss. *Blood Music* is one hell of a ride."

—Moriah LaChapell Schalock, Editor of The Blue Hour Magazine.

"After patching the soles of his boots and washing the dirt from his hands, you'll find Frank Reardon at his typewriter with a rucksack of adventures and fingers itching to scream. In his new book *Blood Music*, Reardon peels back the weathered skin of past love affairs and familial relationships in order to expose the pulsing blood beneath. Never short of breath, the poems in *Blood Music* display modest confidence and genuine vulnerability, creating an organic, visceral collection with a heartbeat of its own."

—Lawrence Gladview, author of *Just Ignore the Beerstains*.

*   *   *

190

"In Blood Music, Frank Reardon's poems are matches set aflame and dropped into the deep well of who we were, who we are, and who we might be, bringing to light all the small moments, the subtle revolutions, and the passing microcosms that we can never get back, save for these fleeting glimpses through poetry like Frank's. Put together, these small moments reveal the sea change happening within all of us, whether we realize it or not. And from these poems, it is clear that Frank is well aware of the passing of time, the importance of final goodbyes, of the next bend in the wooded trail, of one foot placed before the other. It is an excellent collection that speaks honestly and without pretension, which is a rare and valued commodity in days such as these."

—James H. Duncan, editor of The Hobo Camp Review..

Also from Punk Hostage Press –

'Fractured' (2012) by Danny Baker

'Better Than A gun In A Knife Fight' (2012)
            by A. Razor

'The Daughters of Bastards' (2012) by Iris Berry

'Drawn Blood: Collected Works from D.B.P.Ltd., 1985-1995'
(2012) by A. Razor

'impress' (2012) by C.V. Auchterlonie

'Tomorrow, Yvonne- Poetry & Prose for Suicidal Egoists'
(2012) by Yvonne De la Vega

'Beaten Up Beaten Down' (2012) by A. Razor

'miracles of the BloG: A series' (2012)
      by Carolyn Srygley--Moore

'8th & Agony' (2012) by Rich Ferguson

'Untamed' (2013) by Jack Grisham

'Moth Wing Tea' (2013) by Dennis Cruz

'Half-Century Status' (2013) by A. Razor

'Showgirl Confidential' (2013)
   by Pleasant Gehman

Forthcoming from Punk Hostage Press –

'When I Was A Dynamiter' (2013)
      by Lee Quarnstrom

'Dead Lions' (2013) by A.D. Winans

'Yeah, Well...' (2013) by Joel Landmine

'A History of Broken Love Things' (2013)
by SB Stokes

'I Want To Be Your Whore' (2013)
by Alexandra Naughton

'Where The Road Leads You' (2013) by Diana Rose

'Disgraceland' (2014)
by Iris Berry & Pleasant Gehamn

'Long Winded Tales of a Low Plains Drifter' (2014)
by A. Razor

'Shooting for the Stars in Kevlar' (2014)
by Iris Berry

'Dangerous Intersections' (2014) by Annette Cruz

'Driving All of the Horses at Once' (2014)
by Richard Modiano

'Bodies: Brilliant Shapes' (2014) by Kate Menzies

'The Red Hook Giraffe' (2014)
by James Anthony Tropeano III

'Dreams Gone Mad with Hope' (2014)
by S.A. Griffin

'In The Shadow of the Hollywood Sign' (2014)
by Iris Berry

'Puro Purismo' (2014) by A. Razor

www.ingramcontent.com/pod-product-compliance
Lightning Source LLC
LaVergne TN
LVHW041154080426
835511LV00006B/591